WILL HOLDING IN A FART MAKE YOU EXPLODE

QUIRKY QUESTIONS AND INTRIGUING ANSWERS FOR TEENS

LAUREN CLEARWELL

CONTENTS

PART THREE
FOOD—FUN FACTS AND MYTHS

PART FOUR
THE BRAIN AND THE UNEXPLAINED

INTRODUCTION

Alright, let's clear something up before we dive into this weird and wonderful ride. The truth is that you have chosen to read this book because you are a teen with some pretty awesome questions that you are eager to find answers to. Not literally, of course. Granted, these questions might seem a little weird, but even strange questions need real answers!

Your brilliant young mind is likely filled with wonderful questions that could pop into your head when you're trying to avoid doing your homework or even when you're staring at the ceiling. These questions could range from, *Why does my voice sound so weird when it's recorded?* to, *If I hold in a fart, will I explode?* Yes, you're curious, and guess what? That's awesome and part of what makes you uniquely you, and hey, there is no judgment here!

So, let me start off by telling you this: You're not alone. People of all ages sometimes have strange, mind-bending questions, such as, *Why do we laugh when someone trips?* or, *Is it really possible to sneeze with your eyes open?* Let's face it: These are the kinds of questions that might make anyone stop in their tracks and ponder.

Well, the good news is that *Will Holding in a Fart Make You*

Explode: Curious Questions and Intriguing Answers for Teens is your golden ticket to start figuring out the answers to some of the crazy mysteries of life that you can't quite explain. But before you get all *Is this a science textbook?* on me, don't worry; this isn't some boring collection of dry facts. Nope, absolutely not! This book is packed with hilarious answers and everything you need to know about some of the oddities of life. You'll discover some pretty cool things that will make your friends go, "Wait, that's actually true?" or, "Where did you find that out?"

And here's the thing: Being curious is one of the best aspects of being a teenager and a human. So, why not just go with it and fill your mind with knowledge? Choose to be your authentic self and explore all the weird, wonderful, and totally wacky things in life that some people might think about but never dare to speak of or seek the answers to.

It is important to know that asking questions is something that you should be proud of. And guess what? The weirder the question, the better! After all, you're not just any teen; you're a future trivia master. So, buckle up and get ready for one of the weirdest, funniest, and most entertaining rides through some of the strangest questions of life you will ever take.

Whether you choose to read this book for laughs, trivia, or just to impress your friends with mind-blowing facts, it is packed with everything you need. So, go ahead with confidence, be proud of your curiosity, and let's explore some of the world's strange questions and even stranger answers. Let the fun begin!

PART ONE
THE WEIRD AND WACKY HUMAN BODY

WHY ARE PEOPLE SO COMFORTABLE WITH THE SMELL OF THEIR OWN FARTS?

ere's a stinky mystery: Why don't we mind the smell of our own farts? It's as if they've earned VIP status in the world of odors. So, what's going on with this? Well, it all comes down to familiarity. Your body is accustomed to its own natural scents.

When you release a fart, your brain essentially says, *I've smelled worse—this is really no big deal.* This is just part of the whole *being human* experience, much like how you don't mind the smell of your own room, even if it's a little funky, because you're used to it.

But when someone else lets one rip? That's an entirely different story. Your brain doesn't know what's coming and instantly shifts into *What in the world is that?* mode. It's like the difference between hearing your favorite song and suddenly getting blasted with someone else's random playlist. The unfamiliarity hits you like a surprise attack, and your senses really aren't prepared for it.

Farts are made up of gases like nitrogen, oxygen, and carbon dioxide—substances that are completely harmless to you. Since you're the one creating these gases, your brain doesn't see them as a threat. However, when other people fart, their unique chemical mix is less familiar, as if their fart's playlist doesn't quite match your vibe.

In the end, it's all about comfort and familiarity. *Your own farts?* They're just another part of you. *Someone else's?* A plot twist you didn't ask for. But hey, roll with it—it's your own *fragrance*, after all, and you're the creator here!

IS IT POSSIBLE TO SNEEZE WITH YOUR EYES OPEN?

The short answer to this intriguing question is yes, sneezing with one's eyes open is possible. With that said, it is probably important that I add that most people don't try doing this, and the thought likely never crosses their minds either. When you sneeze, your body is essentially performing one big, powerful reset that clears your nose and airways of any unwanted irritants.

Many of the human body's reflexes kick in when you sneeze, including the automatic closing of your eyes. It's a natural response that helps prevent any germs or particles from entering them.

You might try sneezing with your eyes open, but it will likely feel rather uncomfortable. The muscles that control eye movement and blinking are connected to the muscles that you use when you sneeze. So, when you sneeze, the force and pressure can make it nearly impossible to keep your eyes open, at least without genuine effort.

So, do not fret. You are not at risk of your eyeballs popping out when you sneeze. So, while it's physically possible to sneeze with your eyes open, it's probably best to let your eyes shut—after all, your body knows what it's doing!

WHY DO WE HAVE EYEBROWS, AND WHAT'S THEIR PURPOSE?

E yebrows aren't just there to make you look more expressive or to give you the perfect *eyebrow game* on social media. However, let's be totally honest here: That's part of their charm! The main job of eyebrows is actually to protect one of your most precious gifts: your eyes. You can think of them as fancy little shields that direct sweat, water, and dust away from them. It's as if your eyebrows are saying, "Nope, not today, rain!" or, "Keep it moving, sweat!" so that your vision remains crystal clear when you need it the most.

But wait, there's even more! Eyebrows also help you communicate without uttering a word. You might not have realized this before, but it is important to pay attention to eyebrows. They move when a person is shocked, confused, or even deep in thought. Your eyebrows are kind of like your face's very own built-in emoji system. Think about the last time you got a surprise? Did you notice that you raised your eyebrows in amazement? No, that's not just some strange reflex; that's your eyebrows doing their job to help you express yourself better.

And another thing that might surprise you is that your

eyebrows play a very important role in helping other people recognize your face. Yes, you did not read wrong! You have your very own built-in high-tech facial recognition system. Let's face it: No one is going to mistake you for someone else when they spot your signature eyebrow raise!

So, while your eyebrows might not have superpowers, they're certainly more useful than just being stylish. They're the quiet little heroes of your face—protecting your eyes, expressing your emotions, and making sure people know it's you!

WHY DO WE DREAM, AND DO THEY HAVE HIDDEN MEANINGS?

Dreams. Are they an adventurous exploration of your subconscious mind or just your brain having a late-night party? Honestly, no one really knows. What we *do* know is that dreams are basically your brain's way of sorting through the chaos of the day, except instead of doing it neatly, it scrambles everything together, and suddenly, you're riding a unicorn at top speed through a crowded grocery store.

But dreams aren't just about some interesting storylines; they help you process emotions, memories, and all the random stuff going on in your head. It's like your brain deciding: *Alright, it's time to clean up!*—only instead of organizing things properly, it turns your stress into a full-blown action movie where you're the main character.

So, do dreams actually *mean* anything? Some researchers think they help you deal with unresolved feelings. So, if you dream about showing up to school in nothing but your favorite glow-in-the-dark underwear, maybe your brain is trying to tell you that you're way more stressed than you should be. Or maybe it's just messing with you.

Other people think dreams are just your brain's way of

making sense of random thoughts, which would explain why you suddenly find yourself flying a taco-shaped spaceship. Maybe you're feeling adventurous—or maybe your brain just has a strange sense of humor. Either way, whether your dreams have a hidden meaning or not, they definitely make sleep more interesting. Just don't overthink that one where a giant pancake is chasing you.

WHAT'S MORNING BREATH?

Ah, you are likely familiar with morning breath. I guess one could say that this is one of most people's least favorite parts of waking up in the morning. So, what's really going on in there? Well, to be honest, it's all about bacteria.

When you're fast asleep, your entire body, including your mouth, goes into *rest mode*, and saliva production slows down. This means that while you sleep, there is less of that natural mouthwash to keep things fresh in your mouth, so the bacteria get busy while your mouth rests, feeding on any leftover food particles. The result? That lovely morning breath.

Morning breath might have you feeling a little embarrassed, but it really is not something you should worry about; it's a perfectly normal part of being the remarkable human being that you are! Everyone gets it, even those who proudly proclaim that they have never had bad breath in their lives. The reality is that it's just worse in the morning because the bacteria in your mouth had so many hours to have an unsupervised party while you were asleep, and your mouth didn't get a chance to freshen up.

Now, why does it smell so bad? Well, those hungry

bacteria produce sulfur compounds as they break down any leftover food, and those compounds are what give morning breath that "eewwww" smell. So, if your breath smells like something's died in your mouth, it's just your body's way of saying, *We had a wild night! Thank you!*

Luckily, morning breath is something that you can fix pretty easily by brushing your teeth, using mouthwash, and drinking water when you wake up. So, the next time you wake up with the dreaded morning breath, just remember: It's your body's way of greeting you enthusiastically in the morning with a very unique, *Wake up sunshine! It is time to brush!*

CAN PEOPLE REALLY SPONTANEOUSLY COMBUST?

This is another rather fascinating question. The answer to that question is "no." As cool and possibly terrifying as it might sound in movies, the idea that you could just randomly burst into flames is not something you need to worry about in real life.

Spontaneous human combustion (SHC) is "the notion that someone can suddenly catch fire without any obvious cause," like a freak accident or some unexplained magic. Sounds dramatic, right? However, there is no solid proof that this phenomenon occurs naturally. What might actually be happening in these rare cases is that a small spark or flame ignites the fire, and then, the fat in the human body acts like a giant wick, causing it to burn faster. It's not spontaneous combustion; it's more akin to a BBQ that went horribly wrong, with no one getting invited to the cookout and no marshmallows.

So, don't panic about turning into a human torch while binge-watching your favorite Netflix show. If you feel hot, it's most likely just because you forgot to turn on the fan or air conditioner—not because you're about to suddenly go up in flames. And if you're worried about those candles or lighters that are lying around the house, it's a good idea to put this book down for a second and move them safely out of reach. Other than that, you're far more likely to get a terrible sunburn than to spontaneously combust.

WHY DO VOICES SOUND PECULIAR ON RECORDINGS?

Have you listened with curiosity to a recording of your voice and thought, *Who on Earth is that?* If not, it is high time you did so because you are going to be blown away—not literally, of course. Listening to your own voice on a recording can feel like you're hearing a total stranger talking back to you. If it does, don't worry; you're really not going crazy at all. Your voice does sound different on recordings, and it's actually kind of funny when you think about it.

But why does that happen? Well, when you speak, your voice travels to your ears in two ways. First, just as you would expect it to, there's the sound that travels through the air. Then, there's also the sound that comes from within your head! Yes, you did read that right—from inside your head. While you don't necessarily realize it, your skull vibrates, and those vibrations carry a richer, deeper version of your voice to your inner ear. So, when you hear yourself, it's like you're getting a special VIP pass to the *full, deluxe edition* of your very own voice.

When you listen to a voice recording of yourself, the microphone only picks up the sound coming from outside your head—the air version. There are no additional skull vibrations and no extra depth. This is why your recorded voice often sounds a little higher-pitched or thinner than what you're used to hearing. You're essentially hearing the *radio version* of yourself, not the 3D immersive version you experience in real life.

Guess what? Microphones also have their own unique quirks. They might exaggerate certain parts of your voice, like your high notes or that peculiar sound you make when you say the word *squirrel*. That's why recordings can sometimes make you sound like a completely different person, leading you to wonder, *Is that really me?* So, the next time you cringe at the sound of your own voice on a recording, just remember: It's not you; it's science—and maybe the mic just isn't a fan of your unique vocal range!

WHAT IS HAPPENING WHEN YOUR FOOT GOES TO SLEEP?

Have you ever been sitting for a while and suddenly felt like your foot had become a weird, numb, silly blob that does not belong to you? You try to move it, but it's as if it has decided to take a nap without getting your permission first. So, what's really happening when your foot falls asleep?

Well, it's really not some mystical kind of sleep; it's more like your foot is throwing a little tantrum of its own because it's not getting the attention it needs. This occurs when you put pressure on certain nerves or blood vessels. This usually happens when you sit in an awkward position or cross your legs. When that pressure builds up, it can cut off the blood flow and interfere with the nerve signals going to your foot. Your brain starts receiving the wrong messages, and that's when you start feeling that weird tingling sensation we all know and might even love in some sort of peculiar way.

That sensation is called paresthesia. It's your body's way of telling you, *Hey, I've been deprived of oxygen and nutrients for a bit too long; can you please move so I can wake up?* When you finally shift your position and allow the blood to flow back to your foot, the nerves start firing properly again, which is why you feel the *pins and needles* sensation. It's as if your foot is saying, *Yay, finally, I can feel again!*

So, while it's super annoying, it's really just your body being dramatic. The good news is, it's harmless—just a little reminder from your foot to give it some love and avoid sitting in that uncomfortable position for too long.

WHY DO SNEEZES FEEL SO GOOD?

Have you ever noticed how sneezing feels strangely satisfying? You know that feeling when you've been holding in a sneeze for a bit, and then, *boom*—your body finally gets its moment of glory, and it feels like a mini celebration goes off inside your head. But why does sneezing feel so good? Is it some sort of hidden pleasure that no one told us about?

It turns out that sneezes are like your body's way of hitting the *reset* button. When you sneeze, your body is clearing out irritants—whether it's dust, pollen, or just that random tickle in your nose. But here's the thing: It's not just about getting rid of those irritants. The feeling of relief and release is all part of the fun. Sneezing activates all kinds of muscles in your face, chest, and even your stomach. It's like your body is doing its own mini workout, and you're left with that *ahhh* feeling afterward.

But wait, there's more to this! Sneezing actually releases a burst of endorphins—the same feel-good chemicals that kick in when you exercise or laugh. These endorphins are like your brain's way of giving you a high five after the sneeze is over. It's basically your body's way of saying, *Hey, you did a good job clearing your nose; here's a little reward!*

That's why sneezes sometimes feel so great—you get a quick rush of relief, a boost of endorphins, and, let's face it, a fantastic sense of accomplishment. It's like your body just hit the refresh button on your entire system. So, the next time you sneeze, take a moment to appreciate the tiny celebration your body is throwing just for you. You deserve it!

WHAT'S THE POINT OF GOOSE BUMPS?

You have likely experienced those moments when you get a sudden chill, and your skin erupts in tiny bumps, almost as if your body has turned into a human pincushion. You know, those unmistakable goose bumps? It's as if your body is trying to send a message, but the message is a bit, let's call it, confusing. So, what's the point of these goose bumps anyway?

Well, believe it or not, goose bumps are actually a leftover built-in feature that we have from our furry ancestors. Yep, before we evolved into the smooth-skinned humans we are today, our caveman-like relatives had fur that helped them stay warm and snug and look larger than they were. When they got cold, the hair on their bodies would stand up and trap more air to keep them warm. So, when you get goose bumps, your body is essentially doing its best impression of a chilly, fur-covered ancestor trying to stay cozy—except, uh, we don't have fur anymore.

But goose bumps don't just occur when you're cold! They also appear when you're feeling strong emotions, like fear or excitement, or when listening to an amazing song or story. This is what is known as the fight-or-flight response—your body is preparing for something intense as if you're about to either ace your next science exam or run away from a grizzly bear at Olympic speeds. The tiny muscles situated at the base of your hair follicles contract, and this causes the bumps to form. It's like your body's way of saying, *I don't know if I should be scared, excited, or just super confused, so I'll just go ahead and do this!*

So, while goose bumps don't really have much of a purpose for us anymore, they're a quirky reminder of how unique our bodies are and that they are still holding onto old tricks from the past—and sometimes, just a fun reaction to things that get our emotions buzzing.

WHY DO YOUR FINGERS WRINKLE UP IN WATER?

Spending time relaxing in the pool or taking a long bath can suddenly leave your fingers looking like they're auditioning for a role as an ancient, wise creature in a sci-fi movie. It's as if they change from smooth and sleek to something that truly belongs in a raisin commercial on television rather than on your body. But why does this happen? Is your body just trying to give you a glimpse of what you'll look like when you reach 99 years old? Not quite!

It turns out that wrinkled fingers aren't just a peculiar side effect of spending a little too long in water; there's actually a reason behind it. Your body is getting a little clever here. When your fingers—and perhaps even your toes—wrinkle up in water, it's a response from your body's nervous system. You see, your body is super smart, and believe it or not, this wrinkling might actually help you grip things better. It's like giving your fingers a natural pair of water-resistant gloves!

In the past, scientists believed that the wrinkling was just a result of your skin absorbing water and puffing up in a strange way. However, research now shows that it's actually a rather clever survival trick. The wrinkles create more surface area, which helps your hands grip wet, slippery objects—kind of like the tread on a tire. Cool, right? So, if you were a caveman trying to gather food in a wet environment, your wrinkled fingers would give you a better grip on rocks, plants, or whatever you were trying to grasp.

While we might not need it for survival today, it's still a quirky little reminder of how our bodies used to adapt. And let's be real: Who doesn't enjoy a good wrinkled finger moment to feel extra interesting at the pool or after a bath?

WHAT'S THE REAL PURPOSE OF THE UVULA?

The what? Well, you know that little *dangly* thing that swings around right at the back of your throat when you say, *Ahh*? Yep, that's called the uvula—and no, it's not just there to look like a weird ornament or to make you sound funny when you try to sing. So, what's the real purpose of this mysterious little piece of flesh that's just hanging out in your throat?

Well, believe it or not, the uvula actually has a pretty important job to do. It's not just there to embarrass you when you try to speak in public or to make you self-conscious about the way you look when you yawn. One of its main jobs is to help with swallowing, specifically preventing food and liquids from going up your nose. You know, like that one time you tried to drink something and accidentally shot it out of your nose? Yeah, that's the uvula at work, making sure that doesn't happen—most of the time, at least.

But that's not all! The uvula also helps with speech by assisting in the way you pronounce certain sounds. It helps control the airflow and vibrations in your mouth and throat, making it a crucial part of speaking clearly. It's like the unsung hero of your vocal cords, quietly doing its job so you can chat away without sounding like a mess.

So, while it might seem like a random little blob of something just hanging out, your uvula is actually a key player in swallowing, speaking, and ensuring that you don't accidentally inhale your dinner. It's the unacknowledged champion of your throat, doing its thing without ever asking for a thank you!

IS THERE A SCIENTIFIC REASON BEHIND BEING TICKLISH?

So you're reading a great book, totally relaxed, when suddenly, someone pokes you in the ribs. Instantly, you twist and burst into uncontrollable laughter. What just happened? You were hit by ticklishness.

Science tells us there are two kinds of tickles. *Knismesis* is the light, tingly feeling—like a bug landing on you or a feather brushing past. It might make you squirm a bit, but it usually doesn't make you laugh hard. Then, there's *gargalesis*, the kind that makes you erupt into laughter when someone tickles your ribs, feet, or underarms.

When you get tickled, your skin sends signals straight to your brain, which quickly decides if the sensation is dangerous or just playful and triggers your laugh-and-wiggle response. Try tickling yourself, and nothing happens—your brain already knows what you're about to do and stops the reaction.

Some scientists think ticklishness is a survival trick since your most vulnerable spots are also the most ticklish. Others say it's all about bonding—babies laugh when their parents tickle them, and friends have tickle fights just for fun. In short, ticklishness is your brain's strange way of keeping you safe and making you laugh, even if it sometimes drives you a little crazy.

WHAT'S HAPPENING WHEN YOUR EARS SUDDENLY POP ON A PLANE?

The ear pop—the feeling that makes you want to shove your head into a pillow until it stops. You're cruising at 30,000 ft, enjoying your in-flight snack, and suddenly: pop! All of a sudden, your ears feel like they've been expertly plugged with cotton. *What's going on in there? Are your ears breaking? Are they secretly holding a grudge against you?*

Nope, it's just your body doing its thing to keep you comfortable, even if it feels a little weird. When you're flying, the air pressure inside the airplane cabin changes as you gain altitude or descend. Your ears are like tiny pressure-sensitive monitors, and when the pressure inside the cabin doesn't match the pressure inside your middle ear, your eardrum stretches to try to equalize everything. This results in that popping sound—and honestly, it's just your body trying to maintain balance.

Normally, your ears are pretty good at managing this. Your *Eustachian tubes* are "those tiny passageways that connect your middle ear to the back of your nose and throat, and help regulate the pressure." But sometimes, especially if you're sick, congested, or just flying at high speed, those tubes can become a little blocked. That's when you'll feel that pressure building up, and you'll need to pop your ears.

To help speed up the process, you can try swallowing, yawning, or gently blowing out while pinching your nose. Remember not to blow too hard, though—there's no need to create a pressure crisis. This helps your Eustachian tubes open up and balance the pressure.

So, while ear popping may sound a bit dramatic, it's actually just your body's way of saying, *I've got this—let me take care of the pressure.* If only the snacks on the plane were as good at handling it as your ears are!

CAN YOU SWEAT SO MUCH THAT YOU SLIP ON YOUR OWN BODY?

This might sound like something that only happens in hilarious cartoons, but if you've ever survived gym class on a hot day, you *know* the struggle. One second, you're crushing those burpees, and the next—*whoop!*—your hand slips out from under you like you just stepped on a bar of soap made out of… well, you.

So, what's going on? Firstly, if you are human, you perspire! Sweat levels can vary a lot from person to person, but on average, most people lose between 0.5–2 L of sweat per hour when exercising. Even on chill, barely-moving days, your body can still release around 3 L—just from existing. So yeah, even doing very little physical activity can make you leak like a slow-drip faucet.

Most of the time, your clothes soak it up, or it just evaporates. But if you're shirtless, barefoot, or working out on a smooth surface, slipping in your own sweat is actually possible. Not common—but definitely possible.

Now, if you're someone who sweats a *lot*, even when you're not moving much, you might have something called hyperhidrosis. That's just a fancy name for excessive sweating that happens when your sweat glands don't know when to quit. It's totally real, kind of frustrating, and yeah, it can crank your slip risk way up. People with hyperhidrosis are known to soak through shirts and shoes and, once in a while, leave little puddles behind.

So, can you slip on your own body? Yes, it is not something that happens every day, but it's definitely not a myth, especially if your body's in full sprinkler mode. Just one more reason to bring a towel and perhaps even rethink doing push-ups on surfaces that you can slip on when they are wet.

PART TWO
STRANGE REACTIONS AND EVERYDAY ODDITIES

WHY DO WE LAUGH WHEN SOMEONE FALLS OVER?

Someone trips, stumbles, or takes a nosedive, and suddenly, you're doing your very best not to burst out laughing. It's as if your body just can't help itself, even if you're worried they might be hurt. *So, why do we laugh when someone falls over? Are we secretly all just sadistic, or is there something deeper going on here?*

Well, it turns out there's a psychological reason behind it, and it's not because you're evil. When someone falls, it triggers something called *incongruity theory*—basically, our brains find it funny when things don't go as expected. In our everyday lives, we're accustomed to seeing people upright and walking around like normal humans. So, when someone takes a tumble, it's an unexpected moment, and our brains find that surprising, even though we know it's probably harmless. It's like your brain's way of saying, *Whoa, that was totally not supposed to happen… but it did. And now, I don't know how to react, so I'll just laugh it off.*

But here's the funny part: We also laugh because we're relieved. When someone falls, there's that tiny split second when we all think, *Oh no, are they okay?* But if they pop right back up as if nothing happened, the relief floods in, and we can't help but laugh at the silliness of it all. It's almost as though laughing is our body's way of letting go of the tension that came with the fall.

So, while it might seem like we're all just heartless gigglers, laughter is actually a natural reaction to a mix of surprise, relief, and, honestly, the sheer ridiculousness of watching someone suddenly become part of the floor. Just remember to check if they're okay first—then, you can giggle without feeling guilty.

WHY DO MOSQUITOES THINK YOU'RE A FIVE-STAR SNACK WHILE EVERYONE ELSE GETS A PASS?

Nature's very own tiny, buzzing vampires that can't seem to get enough of some people's blood: the infamous mosquitoes. You're just chilling outside or inside, and suddenly, *zap!* Someone else is getting attacked while you're left in peace. *Why do mosquitoes prefer some people over others? Are they just bad at making friends, or is there a method to their buzzing madness?*

Well, it turns out mosquitoes are a bit picky about their dining choices. They're not randomly choosing who to snack on; they have preferences, and those preferences are actually backed by science. First of all, mosquitoes are attracted to carbon dioxide, which is something that we all breathe out. So, if you're breathing like a marathon runner after just a few sprints, you might be a prime target. But it's not just about how much air you're expelling; mosquitoes also love certain scents produced by your skin and sweat. Substances like lactic acid, uric acid, and ammonia—yum, right?—can make you smell like a five-star mosquito buffet.

But wait, there's more! If you've got a higher body temperature or produce more body heat, mosquitoes are basically drawn to you like a moth to a flame. So, if you're always the warmest person in the room or have naturally sweaty feet, congratulations! You're probably the VIP of the mosquito world.

And here's a fun fact: Some people naturally produce more of the stuff mosquitoes love, while others are like an *all-you-can-eat buffet* for mosquitoes. It's not personal; mosquitoes just have their preferences, and unfortunately, some of us are walking, buzzing mosquito magnets.

So, next time you're outside and everyone else is being attacked while you sip your iced tea in peace, just remember: It's not that you're better than everyone else; it's just that you're a little less delicious to mosquitoes. Lucky you!

WHY DO OUR STOMACHS GROW LOUDEST WHEN WE'RE QUIET?

Another moment of embarrassment: the unexpected tummy growl. You're hanging out with your friends, or maybe you're in class, and then suddenly—*boom*—your stomach decides to make an entrance, sounding like it's auditioning for a role in a jungle documentary. It always seems to happen at the worst possible time, right? So, why does your stomach make this dramatic noise when you're super quiet?

Well, the reason your stomach growls is that it's basically reminding you that it's hungry and waiting for food. When you're quiet, there's less noise to cover up the rumbling from your stomach and intestines, so it becomes much more obvious. Think of it as your body's very own way of saying, *Hey, you, I'm busy working hard here! Can you throw me a snack or something? Anything, please?*

Those growls occur when your stomach and intestines are trying to process food, even if there's nothing in there to process. It's like your digestive system gets bored and wants to do a little checkup to make sure everything is still working.

Additionally, it's not just about being hungry. Sometimes, your stomach goes into *check mode* to see if food is coming soon. It's kind of like your stomach is playing the *Let's-see-if-anyone-notices-I-exist* game. Since it usually happens when things are quiet, everyone definitely notices. It's like the sound is much louder when you're in a peaceful moment, especially in class or when you are hanging out with friends.

So, the next time your stomach decides to remind you of its needs and presence, just know that it's really just trying to get your attention. No big deal—everyone's tummies make weird noises sometimes. Just have a chuckle, grab a snack, and move on!

IS EMBARRASSMENT SOMETHING YOU CAN REALLY DIE FROM?

You have likely heard someone in your circle say, "I almost died of embarrassment." You may have also wondered, *Can a person really die of embarrassment?* You know that feeling when you trip in front of your crush or accidentally text the wrong person, causing your face to go from pale to tomato red in 0.5 seconds? It's the worst feeling, right? Naturally, you might wonder: *Can all this embarrassment really be life-threatening?*

Well, relax. No, you can't actually die from embarrassment. While your embarrassment won't cause an immediate *game over* screen, it can have some pretty funny side effects. When you're embarrassed, your body goes into full-on stress mode. Your heart starts racing, your face turns red, and you might even start sweating or feel like you're about to faint. It's as if your body is saying, *Uh... oh, this is a rather awkward moment; let's respond to this situation like it's a matter of life or death.* But in reality, it's just you trying to survive a social disaster, not experiencing a heart attack.

The reason we feel like we're about to die when we're embarrassed is that our bodies respond to embarrassment in the same way they do when we are anxious or scared. And you guessed right, this is the *fight-or-flight* response. Instead of running away from a bear, you're trying to escape from the emotional bear known as social awkwardness. Your body pumps out adrenaline and cortisol, which are stress hormones that make you feel jittery, flushed, and ready to melt into the floor.

But no worries! Even though it feels like your social life is crumbling in real-time, it's unlikely that a little embarrassment will end your life unless it causes you not to seek medical help when you need it. You'll live to tell the tale after the occasional embarrassing moment—and probably laugh about it later. Just remember: Everyone's been there, and your embarrassing moment will be forgotten much faster than you think it will.

WHY DO SOME PEOPLE GET HANGRY?

angry is that magical combination of *hungry* and *angry* that turns even the nicest person into a snack-demanding, short-tempered monster on the attack. You've probably seen it before: Someone's in a perfectly good mood, but once their stomach starts growling, it's as if a switch flips, and suddenly, they're a totally different person. So, why do people get hangry?

Well, it's all due to your body's internal drama. When you haven't eaten in a while, your blood sugar drops, and that's when things can get a little wild. Your brain needs sugar—glucose—to function properly, and when it doesn't get the energy it desires, it sends out a signal to make you, well, not a very pleasant person to be around. Your body releases stress hormones like adrenaline and cortisol, which are normally there to help you deal with danger, but in this case, they're just making you irritable because food is the danger. And guess what? That grumpy mood that you're suddenly experiencing? It's your body's way of motivating you to find food as soon as possible.

Basically, your brain is saying, *Hey, I'm super hungry, and I'm not having a good time right now, so I'm going to make sure you're in a bad mood until you fix this situation.* It's like a little emotional hostage situation where only food can save you. Furthermore, hunger can impede your ability to think clearly, making it much harder to make decisions when you're hangry. Want to argue with someone? Yes, hunger makes it significantly easier to snap at them.

So, the next time someone goes from chill to "I'm about to throw my phone out the window because I'm hungry," just remember that being hangry is a real phenomenon, and it's all about your body's natural need for food. Feed yourself, and watch the transformation back into your regular self!

WHY DO WE YAWN WHEN OTHERS DO?

The yawn is a universal sign that says, *I'm tired, bored, or maybe I'm just trying to be a part of the crowd.* But here's the real question: Why do we always yawn when someone else does? Is it because we're secretly all part of some ancient yawning cult, or is there something else going on?

Well, it turns out that yawning is actually *contagious*, and it's not just because yawns are a sneaky way to get the attention of everyone around you—although that's a pretty good side effect. When we see someone yawn, our brains react by mimicking their actions. It's like an automatic response, similar to how you might smile when someone else smiles.

Scientists call it *contagious yawning*, and it can be all about social bonding. Yup, you read that right: When you yawn in response to someone else, your brain is connecting with theirs in a weird but totally human way. It's like your brain's unique way of saying, *It's okay, I get you, bro.*

But why does it happen? Research suggests that contagious yawning is linked to empathy. When we see someone else yawn, our brains recognize it and *feel* it—sort of like we're sharing the same emotion or tiredness. So, if your friend yawns, you might think, *Hey, yeah, I'm tired, too. Let's yawn together and make this a group effort.* It's actually a sign that we're in tune with the people around us, which is pretty cool when you think about it.

And yes, it's totally contagious. You've probably experienced it yourself—one person yawns, and within seconds, the entire room is caught in a giant yawn chain. It's like a yawn domino effect that you just can't escape. The next time you catch yourself yawning after someone else, just remember: It's not a coincidence; it's social brain magic at work!

CAN YOU BECOME ILL FROM BEING OUTDOORS WITH WET HAIR?

The classic *wet hair equals sickness* myth is something you might have heard from your mom many times while growing up, right? "Don't go outside with wet hair; you *are going to* catch a cold!" It's like an ancient warning passed down through generations, but is there any truth to it? Can you really catch a cold just by stepping outside with damp hair?

Well, the short answer to that is "Nope." You won't actually catch a cold *just* from going outside with wet hair. Colds are caused by viruses—specifically, rhinoviruses—not by the weather or your hair's moisture levels. So, wet hair is not what is going to make you sick, but it will likely have you feeling a little chilly and uncomfortable.

That said, while wet hair doesn't directly cause illness, being cold and uncomfortable could weaken your immune system a little, making you more vulnerable to the viruses that are already lingering around. If you're standing in the cold for a long time, shivering and feeling miserable, that could theoretically give the viruses an easier way to sneak in. But don't worry if you're just running to the store or walking to class with wet hair, your immune system is probably tough enough to handle it.

So, while you're unlikely to wake up with a cold from that wet-hair moment, it's still a good idea to dry off before heading outside if you want to stay warm and comfortable. Plus, there's nothing worse than freezing with cold, wet hair on a windy day. Trust me, your hair will thank you.

IS CRACKING YOUR KNUCKLES BAD FOR YOU?

That notorious knuckle crack—the sound that sends everyone around you into a mini panic attack as if they're about to witness some sort of ancient ritual. You've likely been warned: "Stop cracking your knuckles; you'll get arthritis!" But is that actually true, or is it just another myth designed to make you feel guilty and change your bad habits?

Well, the truth is that cracking your knuckles doesn't cause arthritis. That is a relief, right? The cracking sound you hear is just air bubbles popping in the joints as you stretch them. It's not bones rubbing together or anything creepy like that. The sound is harmless, and there's no reliable scientific evidence that cracking your knuckles leads to arthritis or long-term damage. So, feel free to keep cracking away if you want!

However, like with most things in life, there's a little warning... While cracking your knuckles might not cause arthritis, it can most certainly lead to some other issues that you do not want to deal with. If you're cracking your knuckles frequently, you might irritate the ligaments around the joints or cause some temporary discomfort. If you crack them constantly and aggressively, you could even end up with a little swelling or decreased grip strength. So, if your knuckle-cracking habit is turning into a bit of an obsession, it might be worth taking a break every now and then to give your hands some much-needed rest.

In the end, cracking your knuckles is pretty harmless as long as it doesn't hurt or cause you any discomfort. Just be mindful and remember: It's not the sound that's the problem, but the constant cracking that might lead to a little soreness.

WHAT CAUSES HICCUPS, AND CAN YOU STOP THEM?

Hiccups can possibly be considered many people's least favorite surprise party guest. They just show up out of nowhere, usually at the most inconvenient time, such as in the middle of class or while you're trying to impress someone with your *extremely important* story. So, what's going on when your body decides to randomly start making that weird *hic* sound every few seconds?

Hiccups occur when your diaphragm, the muscle right under your lungs, suddenly spasms. This muscle usually helps you breathe in and out smoothly, but when it spasms, it causes your vocal cords to snap shut, and boom—you get that classic *hic* sound. It's as if your body's having a little hiccup party without inviting you. No one knows exactly why this happens, but it could be triggered by factors such as eating too quickly, drinking carbonated beverages, or even laughing too hard. Some people experience hiccups when they're stressed or nervous as well. Essentially, it's like your body's way of saying, *Surprise! We're going to do this random thing now.*

But how do you stop them? Well, there are numerous

quirky *cures* out there: Some people swear by holding their breath for a few seconds, as if they're about to dive into the world's longest underwater adventure. Then, there are others who even try drinking water upside down or swallowing spoonfuls of peanut butter. Don't ask me why—it just works for some people. Some folks even believe that startling you is the key because, apparently, *nothing stops a hiccup better than a sudden shock.* However, no single cure is guaranteed to work for everyone. It's a bit like a game of *try everything until something finally works!*

So, the next time you're stuck with a hectic case of the hiccups, just remember: It's your body being weird, but it's harmless. And maybe try a few of those hiccup hacks if you're feeling brave! Just don't be surprised if you get even more hiccups from trying too hard to stop them.

WHY DO PEOPLE SOMETIMES JERK AWAKE JUST BEFORE FALLING ASLEEP?

Have you ever experienced that moment when you're about to fall into a peaceful slumber, and suddenly, your body decides to *spasmodically* launch itself awake as if you're on a trampoline? It's like your own personal mini roller coaster that nobody asked for, and it always seems to happen at the worst possible time. But what's going on when your body gives you a *surprise wake-up call* right before you crash into dreamland?

This involuntary wake-up move is called a *hypnic jerk, myoclonic jerk, or sleep start*, and it's completely normal, even though it's still quite strange. It occurs when your body's muscles begin to relax as you fall asleep, but for some reason, your brain panics a little, thinking you're falling or losing control. So, it sends a jolt through your body to wake you up as if you were about to face-plant into the ground. Your brain's like, *Hold up, are we about to fall? Wake up, sleepy soldier!*

The fascinating thing is that nobody truly knows why these jerks happen, but scientists have a few theories. One—previously mentioned—is that when your muscles relax, your brain can get confused and think you're actually falling. Another idea is that it's just a leftover reflex from our ancient ancestors, who needed to wake up quickly in case they were about to fall out of a tree or something. Weird thought: *early humans trying to nap while perched on branches!* Stress or anxiety might make these jerks occur more frequently, too. So, if you're stressing about homework or a big test, your body might be extra jumpy as it attempts to shut down.

The good news? These jerks are completely harmless. It might feel like you're having a mini panic attack right before you sleep, but your body just wants to keep you safe—so, it's like a little "whoa, not today" move before you get too comfy.

So, next time you experience one of these unexpected wake-ups, remember: Your body is just doing its thing, making sure you don't take a nosedive into the pillow *without a plan*.

CAN YOU REALLY FORGET HOW TO WALK?

Unless you're one of the very first bipedal robots, you're probably not going to forget how to walk. Fortunately, as a human being, once you've learned it, your brain tucks that skill away like a favorite playlist on repeat. It becomes automatic—like riding a bike or knowing exactly where the snacks are kept.

The part of your brain that keeps walking smooth and steady is called the cerebellum, and it's in charge of balance and coordination. So, even if you're half-asleep and shuffling to the fridge at 2 a.m., your body instinctively knows exactly what it needs to do—no major thinking required.

But here's the twist: While most people don't just *forget* how to walk, there have been a few rare cases where someone suddenly loses the ability without being hurt. It's called Functional Neurological Disorder (FND), and it's like your brain hits pause, not because it's broken, but because it's overwhelmed or confused. It can happen during times of major stress or anxiety, and it makes moving feel really hard. When this happens, your legs stop cooperating, your balance might become a little off, and you could even fall. It's not fake, and it's usually temporary—but it's very real.

And then, there are those everyday awkward moments like when your foot's asleep or you randomly trip over nothing. Your brain still knows how to walk; your body's just playing catch-up. That's not forgetting—it's being perfectly human.

CAN HUMANS SURVIVE WITHOUT SLEEP?

Sleep: the one thing many people love to complain about not getting enough of. But can humans actually survive without it? Can we just go full-on *no sleep* mode and power through life like we're on some kind of superhero grind? Spoiler alert: *nope*. Humans are not built for that kind of sleepless stunt.

Sleep is like your body's personal reset button. It's when your brain and body get their time to recharge, clean up, and prepare to tackle a new day. Without sleep, things go *south* real fast. In fact, if you try to go without sleep for too long, you'll start to feel like you're living in a walking nightmare. The first thing that happens is that your brain will start to get all fuzzy. It's like trying to run your phone on one percent battery—it'll work for a while, but eventually, it's going to glitch out.

After just a few days without sleep, you'll probably feel more forgetful, have trouble concentrating, and might start seeing things that aren't there at all. Yep, hallucinations. It's as if your brain starts to go a little rogue without that sweet, sweet REM sleep. And, as you can probably guess, without sleep, your body's immune system also goes down the drain, which makes it more likely that you will get sick.

Now, the bad news doesn't stop there. Long-term sleep deprivation can mess with your metabolism and lead to issues like weight gain, higher stress levels, and even serious health problems like heart disease. So, while pulling an all-nighter to finish that last-minute homework might feel like a badge of honor, it's actually doing you far more harm than good.

So, now you know that human beings cannot survive without sleep and should also not try to do so. Sure, we can go for a few days, but it's not pretty. So, the next time you think about skipping out on sleep to stay up late and scroll through TikTok or study, just remember: Your body and brain will let you know it's time for some much-needed rest.

PART THREE
FOOD—FUN FACTS AND MYTHS

CAN EATING TONS OF CARROTS IMPROVE YOUR EYESIGHT?

ave you ever been told to eat your carrots so you can see better? Well, that's not exactly how it works. Carrots are good for you, but they won't give you night vision or turn you into some kind of superhero.

This whole idea actually started way back in World War II. British pilots used radar to spot enemy planes at night, but to keep it a secret, the military spread a rumor that they just ate a lot of carrots. People believed it, and suddenly, everyone thought carrots were magical for eyesight.

Now, carrots are extremely healthy and packed with vitamin A, which helps keep your eyes functioning properly. If you're really low on vitamin A, your vision can deteriorate, especially in the dark. So, while carrots help, they won't enable you to see through walls or find the TV remote any faster.

Instead of bingeing on carrots, if you really want to take care of your eyes, don't spend hours glued to a screen, try not to read in poor lighting, and maybe don't sit 2 in. away from the TV. It turns out parents do have a point sometimes. Also, mix things up: Leafy greens, eggs, and fish are great for your eyes, too.

So yes, carrots are good for you, but they're not a magical cure for 20/20 vision. Eat them because they're tasty, not because you're hoping to see in the dark like cats do.

IF SWALLOWED, WILL CHEWING GUM STAY IN YOUR TUMMY FOR SEVEN YEARS?

Chances are good that you have heard the warning: "Don't swallow your gum! It'll stick in your stomach for seven years!" Sounds horrifying—and you might already have visions of your insides turning into a bubblegum graveyard. But relax; there is really no need to worry. This is just a myth. Your stomach is not going to turn into a gum museum, and you won't wake up one day filled with old, unchewed wads like a walking gumball machine.

Gum is made from a rubbery base that your body can't necessarily break down like it does with regular food. However, that doesn't mean it sets up camp in your stomach for the better part of a decade. Your digestive system is a well-oiled machine, and anything it can't digest, like gum, corn kernels, and that LEGO piece your little cousin ate, just keeps moving through until—yep, you guessed it—it comes out the other end.

Now, before you start swallowing your entire gum stash, let's be real: Gulping down too much at once can cause a blockage. The discomfort and possible pain could lead your parents to take you to the emergency room, and who knows what comes next—which you would not enjoy.

You could think of it a bit like you would a traffic jam—one that is not happening in peak traffic but in your intestines. It's rare, but it has happened, and trust me, you don't want to be the person explaining that to a doctor. So, while one piece won't turn you into a human PEZ dispenser, it's still best to spit it out in the trash... Yes, you heard right... the trash... *not* under your desk, *not* on the sidewalk, and definitely *not* on your friend's shoe. Trust me, your digestive system and other people's sneakers will appreciate it!

WHY DOES HAIR TURN GRAY?

Have you ever noticed gray hair on an older person and thought, *Whoa, how does that even happen?* Perhaps the last time you saw them, their hair was its usual color, and then the next time, it looked like it had lost a battle with time or a tin of paint. This is not something to worry too much about. While it would be pretty cool if it were, gray hair isn't some sign of ancient wisdom being unlocked. It's just your body's way of showing you that it is deciding to retire from its natural hair color.

Here is how your hair color works: Your hair gets its color from melanin, the same pigment that gives your skin its shade. But as you get older, the melanin-producing cells in hair follicles start to slack off—kind of like a phone battery that doesn't last as long as it used to. Less melanin means less color, and eventually, hair turns gray, silver, or even white gray.

But age isn't the only reason this happens. Genetics play a huge role, so if your parents or grandparents happened to go gray early in life, there's a pretty good chance that you might, too.

Sorry, there are no refunds on that one. And while stress

can speed things up a little, failing a math test or forgetting your best friend's birthday won't make your hair turn gray overnight.

The good news? Gray hair is totally normal, and plenty of people manage to rock the look. Plus, at least it won't turn green—unless you mess with too much chlorine. In that case… well, that's a whole different problem!

CAN YOU REALLY GET ADDICTED TO CHOCOLATE?

Whether you love chocolate, prefer something else, or simply don't care about it, have you ever wondered if you could actually become addicted to it? Is it possible to crave it so much that not having a piece would send you into a total meltdown? Well, good news: You're probably not *technically* addicted. However, that doesn't mean chocolate isn't hard to resist when you're in the mood for something sweet.

Chocolate contains a mix of sugar, fat, and a little caffeine, all of which can make your brain feel pretty good. It also contains something called theobromine, which provides a small energy boost. When you eat it, your wonderful brain gets to work and releases dopamine, those *feel-good* chemicals that can make you feel all cozy and happy. So, it makes sense that chocolate might be tempting, especially when you're craving a treat.

But addicted? Not quite, but a person could feel like they could be. Unlike other substances that cause physical dependence, chocolate cravings are more about habit and the enjoyment of eating something tasty that satisfies your taste buds.

Your brain just loves that reward, and let's be real, who doesn't like feeling good after a snack?

If you find yourself reaching for a chocolate bar every single day, maybe try mixing in some other snacks, too. No judgment here—everyone has their go-to snack. Just remember: Enjoying chocolate doesn't mean you're addicted... unless you start sending love letters to a Hershey's bar. In that case, maybe we should talk a bit more about this!

WHAT UP WITH BELLY BUTTON LINT?

Belly button lint—yeah, that strange little fluff that seems to appear out of nowhere, as if it has its own secret life. Ever wondered what's really going on there? Well, brace yourself: It's basically a mix of tiny fabric fibers, dead skin cells, and anything else your belly button decides to collect throughout the day.

Most of the lint comes from your clothes, especially if you wear fuzzy or dark fabrics. As your shirt rubs against your skin, tiny threads break off and somehow end up in your belly button, as if they're on a top secret mission. Add in a little sweat and some skin cells, and boom, you've got yourself a fresh batch of lint.

Here's a fun fact: People with more body hair tend to accumulate more belly button lint. But why? Well, belly hair acts like a funnel, guiding all that fluff straight into your navel, almost like a fiber vortex. Lucky them, huh?

The good news is that belly button lint is totally harmless —unless you're collecting it for... well, reasons we'll leave unexplored. If it completely *grosses* you out, just clean your belly button regularly, and you'll be lint-free for a while. But here's the thing: No matter how much you clean, somehow, someway, the lint always finds its way back. It's like a magic trick you can't escape.

DOES COFFEE REALLY STUNT YOUR GROWTH?

Have your parents told you that drinking coffee could stop you from growing taller? You take one sip too many, and—boom!—your growth spurt is officially canceled. That's just another myth. Coffee doesn't actually shrink you or eliminate your chances of reaching your full height potential in life.

This rumor started long ago when people believed that caffeine weakened our bones and stunted growth. But the truth is, science says otherwise—coffee doesn't interfere with your height. The only factors that can determine exactly how tall you will become are your genetics. So, if you have quite a few tall people in your family, congratulations—you're probably on track to be one of them, too. This is a significant benefit in life, especially when you are trying to reach things in high places.

It is important to remember that while coffee won't stop you from growing, it does contain caffeine, and too much of it can interfere with your sleep. Sleep is crucial for growing bodies because that's when your body does much of its repair and growth. If you're drinking coffee and staying up late every night, you might feel sluggish the next day or—worse—get cranky because you're running on empty.

So, if you love the smell and taste of coffee but worry about your height, don't sweat it—you're good to go. Just remember, it's probably a good idea to hold off on espresso shots like you're an overworked office employee. You'll have plenty of time for that later in life when you're a little taller and more caffeine-tolerant!

WHY DO ONIONS MAKE YOU CRY?

Chopping onions can feel like you've walked straight into an emotional movie scene. One minute, you're calmly slicing away, and the next, bam! Tears are streaming down your face as if you're in the middle of the saddest movie scene ever. But don't stress; onions aren't out to get you. They simply have a built-in defense mechanism that has a peculiar way of targeting your eyes.

So, what's going on with this? Well, when you slice into an onion, you're essentially breaking open its cells, which then release a plethora of chemicals into the air. One of them is syn-Propanethial-S-oxide. Oh, and good luck trying to say that five times in a row, super fast.

Syn-Propanethial-S-oxide turns into a gas that rises and makes its way straight to your eyes. Your body, thinking it's under attack, starts pumping out tears to wash the irritant away. Just like that, your kitchen becomes the set for an emotional tear-jerker.

The onion likely wants to protect itself from being eaten, and, unfortunately, you're the target. But don't panic; you can absolutely fight back! Chilling your onion before cutting it can slow down that chemical reaction, making it less likely for those tears to make a dramatic appearance. Alternatively, if you're feeling extra clever, try slicing the onion under running water to keep the irritating gas away from your eyes.

Or, hey, you can always lean into the drama and let everyone believe you're just *super* emotional about the meal. "Oh, I'm fine… it's just these onions getting to me!"

WHAT NOISE HAS BEEN CROWNED THE MOST EAR-PIERCING SOUND IN HISTORY?

Okay, so each one of us knows someone who is a little loud. Perhaps a sibling who yells across rooms or a friend who laughs like a foghorn. While at times you might think they would, none of them come close to beating the loudest sound ever recorded in history.

The loudest sound ever recorded in history was from a volcano. Yes, you read right. Nature outshouted us. In 1883, a volcano named Krakatoa in Indonesia exploded. When we say exploded, we mean it didn't just go "boom." It detonated with so much force that people 3,000 mi away heard it. That's like hearing a blast in London while you're chilling in New York.

The sound is estimated to have measured around 310 dB. Most people's ears start hurting at around 120 dB, breaking the pain threshold. Krakatoa was so loud that it is believed to have burst eardrums 40 mi away and made the atmosphere shake. Scientists say the pressure wave from the eruption circled the planet 4 times.

Now, here's the serious bit: Krakatoa's eruption caused huge tsunamis, destroyed villages, and more than 36,000 people died. So yes, while it holds the record for the loudest sound, it also reminds us how powerful nature is. It's one of those events that's fascinating and heartbreaking all at once.

Still, if we're just talking about the sound, it was so loud that, had sound been able to travel through space, aliens would've turned their ships around and gone, "Nope. Not today." Wait, what? Sound can't travel in space? Yup!

Sound needs something to move through—like air, water, or even solid stuff. Space doesn't have any of that, so sound can't go anywhere. If Krakatoa had erupted on the Moon? Total silence. The lava would still fly everywhere, but nobody would hear a thing.

PART FOUR
THE BRAIN AND THE UNEXPLAINED

IS DÉJÀ VU A BRAIN GLITCH OR A PEEK INTO A PARALLEL UNIVERSE?

éjà vu is "the sensation that you've experienced a moment before, even though you're 100% sure you haven't." It's as if your brain experiences a small glitch, making you think you're reliving something that is happening for the first time. One second, you're eating a sandwich while sitting in class, and then, out of nowhere, you get this strange feeling: *Wait, I've definitely been in this exact situation before. Sandwich and all.*

So, what's really happening? Scientists believe that déjà vu occurs when the brain's memory systems get a little out of sync. Our memory processing is divided into short-term and long-term systems. It is believed that déjà vu might arise when your brain processes something new as a memory, creating a feeling of familiarity when it shouldn't. It's like when your brain experiences a delay in processing the situation at hand; when it catches up, it mistakenly registers it as something that has happened in the past.

Another theory suggests that déjà vu occurs when the brain detects a similarity between what is happening now and a memory you do not consciously recall. It could be a particular smell, scene, or even a feeling that triggers this false sense of familiarity, causing your brain to think, *I've already been here*.

Although it remains somewhat of a mystery, the fact that déjà vu seems to occur when the brain is processing things out of sync suggests it is more of a hiccup in memory processing rather than a truly mystical experience. So, the next time déjà vu strikes, you can smile and think, *My brain is just flexing its memory muscles a little too hard right now.*

WHY DO WE SEE FACES IN CLOUDS?

Have you ever found yourself staring at a cloud and suddenly thinking, *Is that a face staring back at me?* It's almost as if the cloud has a secret to share—or maybe it's trying to send you a message. But don't worry; it's not a mystical sign or a hidden entity reaching out—it's just your brain doing what it does best!

This phenomenon is called pareidolia, which is a fancy word for the brain's natural tendency to spot patterns in random objects. It's the reason why you might see a face in a rock, a slice of toast, or even a spilled cup of coffee. Faces are important to humans for communication, so over time, your brain has become really good at picking them out—even when they aren't present.

Clouds are made of tiny liquid water droplets or ice crystals, and their shapes are influenced by factors like air movement, density, and temperature, so they are naturally uneven and have all kinds of random shapes. If some of those shapes vaguely resemble eyes, a nose, or a mouth, your brain jumps into action and creatively fills in the rest. Before you know it, that amorphous cloud transforms into a fully-formed face in your mind, and your brain is like, *Yep, that's definitely a face.*

It's almost as if your brain can't resist playing a game of *What do you really see?*

So, the next time you spot a cloud that looks like it's grinning back at you, just remember: It might not be a message from the universe; it is just your brain doing its thing. And if that cloud happens to resemble a famous celebrity, hey, why not have a chat with it?

WHY DO SOME PEOPLE REMEMBER SEEMINGLY POINTLESS FACTS LIKE IT'S A SUPERPOWER?

So, you're talking to someone who casually drops an obscure fact, like the exact number of Jelly Belly jelly bean flavors or the year Napoleon was born, and you're left thinking, *How on Earth do they even remember that?* It's as if their brain is a treasure chest of random knowledge, just waiting to be cracked open at the most unexpected moments.

So, what's the deal with that? Well, it turns out some people are naturally wired to store and recall information that's not necessarily *useful* but is, let's face it, incredibly interesting. Their brains are like super-efficient filing cabinets, with expertly organized quirky facts and details. This skill arises from how their memory systems work, which allows them to encode and retrieve trivia effortlessly. Think of it as a mental collection of oddball knowledge that's just… there.

Another theory is that trivia enthusiasts have a deep passion for learning. They're constantly curious, always on the lookout for new facts, and they take great joy in discovering random tidbits—even if they'll never use them in real life. It's akin to having an encyclopedia of fun facts purely for enjoyment.

So, while you might forget what you had for dinner last week, that trivia champ will be able to recall every single detail about the history of rubber bands. Sure, it might not help in a survival situation, but it certainly makes trivia night unforgettable! This unique skill should be celebrated—it's not just random knowledge but a reflection of a brain that thrives on curiosity, knowledge, and fun.

WHY DOESN'T EVERYONE HAVE A PHOTOGRAPHIC MEMORY?

Do you know someone who can recall every tiny detail from a room they visited years ago or describe a scene from a movie as if it happened yesterday? Meanwhile, you are sitting there trying to remember where you left your favorite book five minutes ago. What's going on?

It turns out that some people are just naturally better at turning their experiences into vivid, almost *photographic* memories. This ability, known as eidetic memory, enables them to recall images, sounds, and details with remarkable accuracy—almost like flipping through a mental photo album. The reality is that true photographic memory is pretty rare. What most of us perceive as perfect recall is actually a mix of impressive memory techniques combined with a brain that is particularly tuned to visual details.

Why does this happen? Part of it is genetic—some brains are naturally better at storing and retrieving images. However, attention, focus, and the amount of effort we put into remembering things also play a major role. If you are someone who consistently takes in the small details around you, your brain is more likely to remember them. Think of it like your brain is a camera that needs to be in the right setting to capture the shot.

If you are not blessed with that *mental camera*, don't sweat it. You can still train your memory to be sharper—just add a little more focus, practice, and perhaps a few memory aids like flashcards. No, we're not all walking around with perfect recall, but remembering where you left your phone or books? That's a victory in its own right!

WHAT'S THE WEIRDEST THING EVER FOUND INSIDE A HUMAN BODY?

Brace yourself—this one's a bit of a roller coaster ride. Over the years, medical doctors have discovered some truly bizarre things inside people's bodies— things that will make you cringe, laugh, and wonder how on Earth they even got there.

One of the most shocking discoveries? A surgical sponge was accidentally left inside a patient after surgery. Yes, a whole sponge was forgotten for years, quietly causing pain without the person knowing it. It wasn't until they under- went another surgery that the doctors found the sponge. Can you just imagine their surprise when it came out? I am certain they must have said something like, "Well, that wasn't supposed to happen."

But that's just the start... There are more! There have been cases of people accidentally swallowing all sorts of things— from hair balls to coins to even toothbrushes. One man ended up with an entire razor blade stuck in his digestive system, and no, I am not sure how that happened either. But that person was one of the unlucky ones, as it has been proven that stomach acids can dissolve razor blades. Spoiler alert: Please, do not try that!

Then, there was the woman who woke up to find a live cockroach in her ear canal. Doctors believed that the roach crawled into the lady's ear while she was sleeping. Definitely not the kind of surprise that anyone would want to wake up to.

Thankfully, these incidents are rare, but they do show just how unpredictable and strange life can be. I guess one could say that the human body can be like a bizarre treasure chest full of oddities. But please, let's stick to food and avoid sharp objects like razor blades.

WHAT STRANGE MEDICAL CONDITIONS HAVE BEEN RECORDED?

The human body has some pretty wild surprises—some conditions are so unusual that they make you wonder if you're living in a sci-fi movie. There are many strange conditions, but for this piece, we are going to look at three in particular.

1. First is hypertrichosis: This is a condition that is sometimes called *werewolf syndrome*. It causes excessive hair growth all over the body—arms, legs, and even the face. Imagine having a beard, hair on your arms, and even on your back all the time! It's rare, but it has been recorded throughout history and is often passed down in families. It might seem strange, but people with hypertrichosis face real challenges, including social stigma and the need for constant care.

2. Next is Cotard's syndrome, a condition in which people believe they are dead or have lost vital organs. It might sound like something out of a horror movie, but it's a serious psychological condition. Those who have it experience deep

distress, believing they are no longer alive, which can make daily life extremely challenging.

3. And don't forget about the person who can't feel pain. No, it's not some kind of superpower; it's a condition called Cognitive Insensitivity to Pain (CIP) in which people do not feel physical pain at all. While it might sound like a gift, it's actually quite dangerous, as pain helps protect us from injuries. Without it, something as simple as a cut could go unnoticed, putting a person at risk of serious harm.

The human body certainly has its quirks. These rare conditions remind us that behind these medical oddities are real people who face unique challenges every day.

WHY DO WE SMELL THINGS THAT AREN'T THERE?

You have probably walked into a room, caught a whiff of something, and thought, *Yummy, fresh popcorn!* only to look around and find no popcorn in sight. Or maybe you catch a hint of roses, but there isn't a flower in the area. Welcome to the strange world of *phantosmia*, where your nose decides to mess with you and sends phantom scents straight to your brain.

So, why does this happen? Our noses are pretty amazing at detecting scents and sending them to our brains. But sometimes, for reasons we still don't fully understand, things can go haywire. It could be a *glitch* in the signal or just an overactive sense of smell making your brain think it detects something when it really doesn't. It is like your brain's scent detector app suddenly going rogue and giving you random *scent suggestions*.

There are several reasons this can happen. It could be something as simple as a cold, allergies, or a sinus infection that messes with your sense of smell. Other times, it's linked to stress or even neurological issues. But in most cases, it's harmless and just another weird quirk of the body.

So, the next time you're convinced you smell something out of nowhere, take a deep breath and laugh it off. It's just your brain playing a quirky game of *What's That Smell?*—and hey, the only thing that's really *off* is your sense of smell!

CAN YOU HEAR SILENCE?

Can you hear silence? This might sound like something right out of a mind-bending movie, but here's the catch: Technically, no, you can't hear silence because it is the absence of sound. However, before you start thinking you are losing touch with reality, let's break it down.

When you find yourself in an incredibly quiet space—think soundproof rooms. Yes, they do exist, and they are a little surreal—you might start to notice something strange: your body's own sounds. Your heartbeat, your breath, and even the sound of blood rushing through your ears. It's as if your brain is still working overtime to process sound, even when the outside world is silent. So, while it feels like silence, you are still hearing your body doing its thing.

In extreme cases, such as in a near-total sound vacuum, people have reported hearing odd, seemingly random noises or feeling as if they have stepped into an entirely different dimension. It can even be a bit unsettling or disorienting as if the silence itself is playing tricks on you. It is almost like by listening too hard to nothing, your mind starts creating its own sounds.

So, can you really hear silence? Not exactly, but you can experience it, and it might end up feeling a lot stranger than you would expect!

WHAT'S THE SCIENCE BEHIND BRAIN FREEZE, AND CAN IT HARM YOU?

You know that feeling when you take a bite of something cold, like ice cream or a slushy, and suddenly, it feels like your brain is doing flips inside your skull? What's happening with this? Is your brain actually short-circuiting? Or is it some cosmic punishment for enjoying another sweet treat?

Don't worry; it's not your brain malfunctioning; it's actually called *sphenopalatine ganglioneuralgia* (Brusie, 2016). Yes, that is a bit of a mouthful, to say the least, but don't let that scare you! What is happening is not nearly as scary as it might seem.

Here's what is happening with this: When something really cold touches the roof of your mouth, it messes with the blood flow in your brain. The blood vessels constrict and then quickly expand, which causes a sharp pain. It's your brain's very unique way of saying, *Whoa, slow down a bit with the cold stuff!*

So, why does this happen? Well, you might not know this, but the roof of your mouth is linked to pain receptors in your head. That is pretty amazing, right? When it gets cold, your brain gets confused and spreads the pain all over your head.

It is kind of like trying to solve a great mystery without having any clues.

The good news? Brain freeze is harmless—it's just a quick, annoying moment. To avoid it, try eating smaller bites or let your cold treat warm up a little before you enjoy it. But if it happens, just roll with it; after all, it's a small price to pay for the sweet joy of ice cream!

PART FIVE
BIZARRE NATURAL PHENOMENA

CAN FISH RAIN FROM
THE SKY?

S o, you might have heard stories about fish falling from the sky. It sounds like something out of a sci-fi movie or a bizarre weather report, right? But hold that thought. Believe it or not, it actually happens—though not in the way you might imagine.

This rare event, known as *fish rain*, occurs "when small aquatic creatures—like fish or frogs—are swept up by powerful storms and later fall back to the ground." But don't worry; it's not a sign of the apocalypse. There's a completely logical, although still pretty weird, explanation.

The most common cause of fish rain is a weather phenomenon called a waterspout. *Waterspouts* are "tornado-like columns of rotating air that form over water." When they become strong enough, they can suck up lightweight objects, including fish, as they pass over lakes, rivers, or oceans. These fish are carried high into the air, sometimes traveling miles before eventually falling back to the ground when the storm loses its strength.

Reports of fish rain date back centuries and have been documented in various parts of the world, including Honduras, where a yearly event called *Lluvia de Peces*—Rain of Fish—has been reported for over 100 years. Amazing, right?

So, while it might seem like a scene from a great fantasy novel, fish rain is a real, though rare, natural occurrence. If you ever find yourself in one, just remember: An umbrella might not be enough to protect you from falling seafood!

WHAT CAUSES "STARRY VISION?"

Have you ever stood up too fast and suddenly felt as if you were inside a glitter explosion? One second, you're fine, and the next, your vision is filled with tiny, twinkling lights. No, you're not unlocking superpowers, and aliens aren't trying to beam you up. What's actually happening is something called orthostatic hypotension—which is just a fancy way of saying that your blood pressure drops too quickly when you stand up.

When you stand up, gravity pulls your blood downward, and your body is supposed to react quickly by tightening blood vessels and increasing your heart rate to maintain sufficient blood flow to your brain. But sometimes, it lags a little, leaving your brain momentarily short on circulation. That's when you experience dizziness, lightheadedness, or those strange, starry flashes—it's basically your body hitting the *please hold* button while it catches up.

Most of the time, your body sorts itself out in a few seconds, and you're good to go. However, if this happens frequently, or if you feel like you might actually pass out, it could be a sign that something else is going on. Dehydration, low blood sugar, certain medications, or underlying health conditions could be causing it. Remember that if this continues to happen, it's worth mentioning to your parents.

So, the next time you stand up too fast and your vision explodes into fireworks, just remember: It's not magic; it's simply your body trying to keep up. There's no need to panic; it's just one of those amusing aspects of being human.

WHAT HAPPENS WHEN YOU
GET A STATIC SHOCK?

The static shock… One moment, you're just going about your day, and the next, *zap!* A tiny jolt that makes you jump as if you've been struck by lightning. *What's going on here?*

What you're feeling is static electricity in action. As you move—whether shuffling across a carpet, pulling off your sweater, or sliding across a car seat—your body picks up extra electrons and builds up an electrical charge. Some materials, like wool, carpet, and synthetic fabrics, are particularly good at transferring these electrons, which is why you're more likely to get shocked in certain situations.

Once your body has built up enough charge, it needs somewhere to release it. The moment you touch something conductive—like a metal doorknob, light switch, or even another person—that stored energy discharges in a quick burst and creates that sharp little shock. It's essentially a mini lightning bolt right at your fingertips.

Static shocks occur more often when you are in dry conditions, especially in winter, because moisture in the air usually helps electricity disperse before it builds up. When the air is dry, those extra charges stick around longer, just waiting for the perfect moment to surprise you.

The good news? Static shocks are pretty harmless—they are just a little zap to remind you that physics is always at work, even when you're not thinking about it. So, the next time you get a shock, don't take it personally. Nature's keeping you on your toes or maybe encouraging you to invest in a good pair of rubber-soled shoes!

WHY DO SOME ANIMALS MAGICALLY GLOW IN THE DARK?

Have you ever been walking around at night in the dark and suddenly spotted a mysterious glow in the distance? Nope, you guessed wrong; it's not a UFO, and you haven't unlocked night vision—it's just nature showing off. Some animals, like fireflies, jellyfish, and certain deep-sea fish, have a built-in ability to glow, thanks to a phenomenon called bioluminescence—nature's very own version of a glow stick!

But why do they do it? Well, glowing serves different purposes depending on the animal, and most of the time, it's for survival, communication, or—believe it or not—romance. For fireflies, glowing is all about attracting the perfect mate. Those twinkling flashes in the night? They're basically firefly love signals. Males send out glowing patterns to impress females, and if a female is interested, she flashes back—like nature's version of texting, *Hey...*

Other creatures, like certain jellyfish and deep-sea fish, use bioluminescence for camouflage. In the darkest depths of the ocean, glowing in the same color as the surrounding light helps them blend in and avoid predators. It's like an invisibility cloak—just so much cooler.

Then, there are animals that use their glow to confuse predators or lure in their prey. Some squids, for example, create pulsating light patterns to distract attackers or attract unsuspecting dinners. It's like the underwater version of a laser show—except with more tentacles and fewer DJs.

But it's not just wild creatures that have this glowing superpower; some household pets also exhibit biolumines-cence! Certain species of cats and dogs, particularly those with glowing fur, can emit a glow under UV light. This glow is due to specific proteins in their skin and hair reacting to ultraviolet light. While this bioluminescence doesn't occur naturally, like it does for fireflies, it's still a fascinating little trick that scientists have discovered in genetically modified animals or under specific light conditions.

So, the next time you see something glowing in nature or your own backyard, take a deep breath and don't panic. It's not an alien invasion—just some incredible creatures showing off their built-in night-lights. Pretty awesome, right?

WHAT'S UP WITH DOGS GIVING THAT SIGNATURE HEAD TILT WHEN LISTENING — IS IT JUST CUTENESS OR SOMETHING ELSE?

H as your dog ever tilted its head when you talk to it as if it's trying to crack some kind of code or solve one of Sherlock Holmes's great mysteries? It's one of the cutest things it does, but what's really going on behind those adorable eyes?

Well, dogs tilt their heads for a few reasons, and it usually comes down to their desire to understand you better or remember something. First, when they tilt their heads, they're adjusting their ears to hear you more effectively. Their ears are incredibly flexible, and tilting their heads helps them fine-tune what they're listening to. It's almost like they're saying, *Wait, what? Please repeat that.* The tilt also helps them figure out where the sound is coming from, much like their own little version of sonar.

But it's not just about hearing. They're also trying to see us better. Dogs are experts at reading our faces and emotions, so when they tilt their heads, they're getting a better view of our expressions. They're trying to determine if we're happy, upset, or if we're just asking them to *sit* again. It's as if they're little furry detectives, picking up on all the clues we give them.

And let's be honest: Sometimes, they're probably just trying to win us over for a treat! *Oh, please give me a snack!* It's their go-to move for getting a little extra love or a tasty reward. So, when your dog gives you that adorable head tilt, just know it's either trying to figure you out, remember something, or—yummy—angling for a treat. Either way, it's too cute to resist!

WILL HOLDING IN A FART REALLY MAKE YOU EXPLODE?

The answer to this question is a giant *no!* While holding in a fart will not make you explode, it might make you wish that you could! When you feel the pressure building, it's because your body is creating gas as part of the digestive process. Every day, your stomach and intestines work hard to break down all that tasty food you eat, which produces gas that, whether you like it or not, eventually needs to be released.

If you hold that gas in, it doesn't magically disappear. Instead, your body reabsorbs the gas, and you might experience some rather unpleasant symptoms, such as bloating, discomfort, or the occasional stomach ache. You can think of it like trying to stuff too many clothes into a suitcase that is way too small—eventually, something will give!

So, while you won't explode from holding in a fart, it can be uncomfortable, and your stomach might feel a little strange. If you are tempted to hold in a fart during an awkward situation, you're probably better off just letting it out. That said, it is preferable to fart when you're alone. If a fart does happen to slip out at the wrong time, don't feel ashamed or turn a shade of crimson red—remember that it's a normal part of digestion, and everyone farts, even those trending social media influencers!

So, don't worry your pretty little head off about some dramatic explosion from holding in a fart, but don't hold it in for too long—your body might find a way to let it out when you least want or expect it to!

AFTERWORD

Well, folks, here we are at the end of this wild, weird, and totally wacky ride. You've learned the answers to some of life's most baffling questions—like why we can't help but laugh when someone trips and why we can't keep a straight face when our own farts are involved. We've dived into everything from the mysterious purpose of your uvula—who knew that was even a thing?—to whether cracking your knuckles really leads to arthritis. Spoiler alert: It won't, but it still might drive the person next to you crazy.

And let's not forget the good stuff—like how holding in a fart won't make you explode. Sure, it might leave you feeling uncomfortable, but you won't turn into a walking time bomb anytime soon. Thank goodness, right? Whether you've been reading through this on a rainy afternoon or using it to dazzle your friends with strange trivia, I hope you've had a few laughs and picked up some fun facts.

Next time you're hanging out with friends and the conversation shifts to "Why does my foot fall asleep?" or "What's the deal with morning breath?" you'll be the one with all the answers and probably some pretty epic jokes to share as well. Congratulations, you've officially earned your *unofficial* PhD in the science of the weird and wonderful questions teens have!

Remember, life's way too short for you to take everything so seriously. So, keep laughing at the little things, keep asking the big questions, and always embrace the weirdness. Until next time, stay fun, curious, and your wonderfully unique self!

And hey, please don't try to hold that fart in... let it go; just maybe do not do so in a crowded elevator!

BIBLIOGRAPHY

Aguirre, C. (2023, October 9). *The science of tickling*. Headspace. https://www.
headspace.com/articles/is-laughter-the-best-medicine

Airplane ear: Symptoms and causes. (2019). Mayo Clinic. https://www.
mayoclinic.org/diseases-conditions/airplane-ear/symptoms-causes/syc-
20351701

Anandanayagam, J. (2024, January 9). *Can you die from embarrassment? What
we know*. Health Digest. https://www.healthdigest.com/1486527/can-
embarrassment-cause-death/

Ask the brains: Why do we laugh when someone falls? (2008). *Scientific American Mind*, *19*(5), 86-86. https://doi.org/10.1038/scientificamerican
mind1008-86

Bad breath: Symptoms and causes. (2018). Mayo Clinic. https://www.
mayoclinic.org/diseases-conditions/bad-breath/symptoms-causes/syc-
20350922

Baraza, B. (2024, December 26). *Science behind why we like our own farts and
what it says about leadership and empowerment*. Medium. https://medium.
com/@Balozi.Baraza/the-science-behind-why-we-like-our-own-farts-
and-what-it-says-about-leadership-and-empowerment-9c7fc9f45298

Beaulieu-Pelletier, G. (2023, March 13). *Why do we laugh when someone falls
down? Here's what science says*. The Conversation. https://theconversation.
com/why-do-we-laugh-when-someone-falls-down-heres-what-science-
says-199367

Bedinghaus, T. (2019). *Understand why you sometimes see stars and flashes of
light*. Verywell Health. https://www.verywellhealth.com/why-do-i-see-
stars-3422028

Begum, T. (n.d.). *The 1883 Krakatau eruption: A year of blue moons*. Natural
History Museum. https://www.nhm.ac.uk/discover/the-1883-krakatau-
eruption-a-year-of-blue-moons.html

Begum, J. (2021, November 10). *11 facts about sneezes and sneezing*. Medicine-
Net. https://www.medicinenet.com/11_facts_about_sneezes_and_sneez
ing/article.htm

Bhandari, S. (2021). *What is déjà vu?* WebMD. https://www.webmd.com/
mental-health/what-is-deja-vu

Bodily functions explained: Goosebumps. (n.d.). Pfizer. https://www.pfizer.com/
news/articles/bodily_functions_explained_goosebumps

Boyle Wheeler, R. (2019). *Slideshow: facts about gray hair: How to care for it and look your best*. WebMD. https://www.webmd.com/beauty/ss/slideshow-beauty-gray-hair-facts

Brazier, Y. (2024, May 24). *Flatulence: Causes, remedies, and complications*. Medical News Today. https://www.medicalnewstoday.com/articles/7622

Breyer, M. (2025, March 27). *8 reasons mosquitoes are attracted to you*. Verywell Health. https://www.verywellhealth.com/reason-mosquitoes-bite-some-people-more-others-4858811

Brown, H. (2014, January 18). *7 fun and unusual facts about the human body*. Famous Scientists. https://www.famousscientists.org/7-fun-and-unusual-facts-about-the-human-body/

Brusie, C. (2016, December 22). *Sphenopalatine ganglioneuralgia: Guide to brain freeze*. Healthline. https://www.healthline.com/health/sphenopalatine-ganglioneuralgia-brain-freeze

Cahn, L. (2019, November 11). *11 craziest things found in people's bodies*. Reader's Digest. https://www.rd.com/list/craziest-things-found-in-peoples-bodies/?__cf_chl_tk=iFOSpzvXvMLUKSt6LpaHjAVHL0rRM7KP8uKRSu NIqbA-1743597594-1.0.1.1-_ZACmYon641c91nUu2qMyN_7yDOaZfXEKv S8DwHpxsE

Can you sneeze with your eyes open? (2016, December 21). Wonderopolis. https://www.wonderopolis.org/wonder/can-you-sneeze-with-your-eyes-open

Chan, K. (2024, January 8). *Eidetic memory: The reality behind the "photographic" mind*. Verywell Mind. https://www.verywellmind.com/eidetic-memory-7692728

Choi, C. Q. (2013, January 9). *Why fingers & toes get pruney in water*. Live Science. https://www.livescience.com/26097-why-fingers-pruney-water.html

Choi, C. Q. (2023, March 18). *Why do dogs tilt their heads?* Live Science. https://www.livescience.com/why-do-dogs-tilt-their-heads

Cirino , E. (2018, March 1). *Why do we have eyebrows: Functions, thick, thin, and more*. Healthline. https://www.healthline.com/health/why-do-we-have-eyebrows

Dargel, C. (2022, September 20). *Can wet hair make you sick?* Mayo Clinic Health System. https://www.mayoclinichealthsystem.org/hometown-health/speaking-of-health/can-wet-hair-make-you-sick

Edwards, M. J., & Bhatia, K. P. (2012). Functional (psychogenic) movement disorders: Merging mind and brain. *The Lancet Neurology, 11*(3), 250-260. https://doi.org/10.1016/s1474-4422(11)70310-6

Extance, A. (2016, December 21). *Explainer: The chemistry of farts*. Chemistry World. https://www.chemistryworld.com/news/explainer-the-chemistry-of-farts/2500168.article

Fastrich, G. M., Kerr, T., Castel, A. D., & Murayama, K. (2018). The role of interest in memory for trivia questions: An investigation with a large-scale database. *Motivation Science, 4*(3), 227-250. https://doi.org/10.1037/mot0000087

Franzen, A., Mader, S., & Winter, F. (2018). Contagious yawning, empathy, and their relation to prosocial behavior. *National Library of Medicine, 147*(12), 1950-1958. https://doi.org/10.1037/xge0000422

Frothingham, S. (2019, February 12). *What is belly button lint and what should I do about it?* Healthline. https://www.healthline.com/health/belly-button-lint

Frothingham, S. (2020, February 27). *Can you sneeze with your eyes open? Will you hurt yourself?* Healthline. https://www.healthline.com/health/can-you-sneeze-with-your-eyes-open

Galan, N. (2017, August 9). *What is paresthesia? Causes and symptoms.* Medical News Today. https://www.medicalnewstoday.com/articles/318845

Gallup, A. C., & Wozny, S. (2022). Interspecific contagious yawning in humans. *National Library of Medicine, 12*(15), 1908. https://doi.org/10.3390/ani12151908

Ghose, T., & Zimmermann, K. A. (2012, December 11). *Pareidolia: Seeing faces in unusual places.* Live Science. https://www.livescience.com/25448-pareidolia.html

Giorgi, A. (2015, September 26). *Everything you need to know about hiccups.* Healthline. https://www.healthline.com/health/hiccups

Good question: Why does sneezing feel so good? (2012, April 18). *CBS News.* https://www.cbsnews.com/minnesota/news/good-question-why-does-sneezing-feel-so-good/

Gotter, A. (2018, March 26). *Morning breath: Prevention, causes, treatment, and more.* Healthline. https://www.healthline.com/health/morning-breath

Gray, R. (2022, June 20). The surprising benefits of fingers that wrinkle in water. *BBC.* https://www.bbc.com/future/article/20220620-why-humans-evolved-to-have-fingers-that-wrinkle-in-the-bath

Grucza, A. (2022, April 9). *What is congenital insensitivity to pain?* WebMD. https://www.webmd.com/children/what-is-congenital-insensitivity-pain

Gupta, P. (2021, September 30). *Why does sneezing feel good?* LifeMD. https://lifemd.com/learn/why-does-sneezing-feel-good

Hunter, A. (2023, October 11). *Can you sneeze with your eyes open?* HowStuffWorks. https://science.howstuffworks.com/science-vs-myth/everyday-myths/sneeze-with-eyes-open.htm

Johnson, J. (2024, October 21). *Yawning: Causes and reasons for contagious yawning.* Medical News Today. https://www.medicalnewstoday.com/articles/318414

Khan, M. (2008, April 2). *How to keep your stomach quiet in public.* WikiHow. https://www.wikihow.com/Keep-Your-Stomach-Quiet-in-Public

Komarla, J. (2023, December 14). *Why do some people like the smell of their own farts?* ZME Science. https://www.zmescience.com/feature-post/health/food-and-nutrition/why-do-some-people-like-the-smell-of-their-own-farts/

Krakatoa: Eruption, causes & impact. (2018, May 9). History. https://www.history.com/articles/krakatoa

Kumar, M. (2024). Exploring dreams and analyzing its impact on behaviour. *Research Gate, 12*(1). https://doi.org/10.25215/1201.226

Lazear, R. (2025, March 3). *How are clouds' shapes made? A scientist explains the different cloud types and how they help forecast weather.* The Conversation. https://theconversation.com/how-are-clouds-shapes-made-a-scientist-explains-the-different-cloud-types-and-how-they-help-forecast-weather-247682

Love, S. (2023, July 10). *Do we actually "hear" silence?* Scientific American. https://www.scientificamerican.com/article/do-we-actually-hear-silence/

Lovering, N. (2022, June 22). *Can I be addicted to chocolate?* Psych Central. https://psychcentral.com/lib/does-chocolate-addiction-exist

Malchik, A. (2022, August 31). *The bumpy road to a walking robot.* Medium. https://antoniamalchik.medium.com/the-bumpy-road-to-a-walking-robot-c3d5e25e716c

Manto, M., Bower, J. M., Conforto, A. B., Delgado-García, J. M., da Guarda, S. N. F., Gerwig, M., Habas, C., Hagura, N., Ivry, R. B., Mariën, P., Molinari, M., Naito, E., Nowak, D. A., Oulad Ben Taib, N., Pelisson, D., Tesche, C. D., Tilikete, C., & Timmann, D. (2011). Roles of the cerebellum in motor control—the diversity of ideas on cerebellar involvement in movement. *The Cerebellum, 11*(2), 457-487. https://doi.org/10.1007/s12311-011-0331-9

Marks, H. (2012, August 23). *Dreams.* WebMD. https://www.webmd.com/sleep-disorders/dreaming-overview

Mayo Clinic Staff. (2022, May 26). *Orthostatic hypotension (postural hypotension).* Mayo Clinic. https://www.mayoclinic.org/diseases-conditions/orthostatic-hypotension/symptoms-causes/syc-20352548

McCallum, K. (2022, June 3). Why are mosquitoes attracted to some people more than others? *Houston Methodist Leading Medicine.* https://www.houstonmethodist.org/blog/articles/2022/jun/why-are-mosquitoes-attracted-to-some-people-more-than-others/

McDermott, A. (2016, December 20). *Why are people ticklish?* Healthline. https://www.healthline.com/health/why-are-people-ticklish

Microphone technique and choosing a vocal microphone for live performance purposes. (n.d.). SingWise. https://www.singwise.com/articles/microphone-technique-and-choosing-a-vocal-microphone-for-live-performance-purposes

Mir, A. (2024, November 3). *Why do some animals glow? The secrets of biolumi-*

nescence. Medium. https://medium.com/the-thinkers-point/why-do-some-animals-glow-the-secrets-of-bioluminescence-2c91fa02bc02

Mitchell, C. (2019). *Avoiding static electricity fires while pumping gas during winter.* AccuWeather. https://www.accuweather.com/en/weather-news/what-causes-that-annoying-static-shock/338462

Moore, K. (2015, October 6). *Why does my stomach growl?* Healthline. https://www.healthline.com/health/abdominal-sounds

Morgan, K. K. (2024, February 8). *Causes of excessive sweating.* WebMD. https://www.webmd.com/skin-problems-and-treatments/hyperhidrosis-causes-11

Mulcahy, L. (2023, September 12). Why you might not like your recorded voice and how you can change it. *Washington Post.* https://www.washingtonpost.com/wellness/2023/09/12/why-your-recorded-voice-sounds-different/

Myth or fact: Eating carrots improves eyesight. (2013, August 27). *Duke Health.* https://www.dukehealth.org/blog/myth-or-fact-eating-carrots-improves-eyesight

Myth or fact: It takes seven years to digest chewing gum. (2013, August 27). *Duke Health.* https://www.dukehealth.org/blog/myth-or-fact-it-takes-seven-years-digest-chewing-gum

Myths about your eyes and vision. (2024, February 13). WebMD. https://www.webmd.com/eye-health/fact-fiction-myths-about-eyes

Naftulin, J. (2018, June 13). *Why we get hangry, according to science.* Health. https://www.health.com/nutrition/what-is-hangry

Nall, R. (2015, March 9). *Numbness of foot.* Healthline. https://www.healthline.com/health/numbness-of-foot

Nichols, H. (2018, June 28). *Dreams: Causes, types, meaning, what they are, and more.* Medical News Today. https://www.medicalnewstoday.com/articles/284378

Orf, D. (n.d.). *The loudest known sound was the eruption of the Krakatoa volcano.* History Facts. https://historyfacts.com/science-industry/fact/the-loudest-known-sound-was-the-eruption-of-the-krakatoa-volcano/

Osborn, C. (2017, May 8). *26 Remedies for Hiccups.* Healthline. https://www.healthline.com/health/how-to-get-rid-of-hiccups

Palermo, E. (2013, July 1). *Lluvia de Peces: When fish rain from the sky.* Live Science. https://www.livescience.com/37820-lluvia-de-peces-fish-rain.html

Panoff, L. (2019, June 5). *Are carrots good for your eyes?* Healthline. https://www.healthline.com/nutrition/are-carrots-good-for-your-eyes

Pappas, S. (2023, February 1). *What causes déjà vu?* Scientific American. https://www.scientificamerican.com/article/what-causes-the-feeling-of-deja-vu/

Pareidolia. (2023). Psychology Today. https://www.psychologytoday.com/za/basics/pareidolia

Rajan, E. (2019, December 31). *Swallowing gum: Is it harmful?* Mayo Clinic. https://www.mayoclinic.org/diseases-conditions/indigestion/expert-answers/digestive-system/faq-20058446

Rath, L. (2022, February 13). *Cotard's Syndrome: What is it?* WebMD. https://www.webmd.com/schizophrenia/cotards-syndrome

Roland, J. (2017). *Hypertrichosis (Werewolf Syndrome): Causes, treatments, and types.* Healthline. https://www.healthline.com/health/hypertrichosis

Rosa-Aquino, P. (2022, December 17). *Strange reports have claimed humans spontaneously burst into flames, but science can explain how bodies sometimes act like a candle wick.* Business Insider. https://www.businessinsider.com/is-spontaneous-human-combustion-real-or-myth-scientific-evidence

Sadr, J., Jarudi, I., & Sinha, P. (2003). Role of eyebrows in face recognition. *Sage Journals, 32*(3), 285-293. https://doi.org/10.1068/p5027

Santos-Longhurst, A. (2018, July 30). *How long does gum take to digest?* Healthline. https://www.healthline.com/health/how-long-does-gum-take-to-digest

Semple, K. (2017, July 16). Every year, the sky "rains fish." Explanations vary. *The New York Times.* https://www.nytimes.com/2017/07/16/world/americas/honduras-rain-fish-yoro.html

Shmerling, R. H. (2018, May 6). Knuckle cracking: Annoying and harmful, or just annoying? *Harvard Health Blog.* https://www.health.harvard.edu/blog/knuckle-cracking-annoying-and-harmful-or-just-annoying-2018051413797

Shmerling, R. H. (2020, August 3). Wondering about goosebumps? Of course you are. *Harvard Health Blog.* https://www.health.harvard.edu/blog/wondering-about-goosebumps-of-course-you-are-2020080320688

Sinclair, C. (2022, May 24). Hearing protection at festivals and concerts. *Alpine Hearing Protection.* https://www.alpinehearingprotection.com/blogs/party-music/hearing-protection-at-festivals-and-concerts

Singh, N. (2022, April 10). *Scientists found why people like the smell of their own farts.* Medium. https://medium.com/illumination/experts-found-people-like-the-smell-of-their-own-farts-7193c05ba764

Smuts, A. (n.d.). *Humor.* Internet Encyclopedia of Philosophy. https://iep.utm.edu/humor/

Sneeze can travel up to 100 mph! (2022). American Renaissance School. https://www.arsnc.org/2022/12/16/7218/coughing-and-sneezing-are-just-some-of-the-more-interesting-and-complicated-ways-the-body-works-to-protect-your-lungs-from-contamination

Songu, M., & Cingi, C. (2009). Sneeze reflex: Facts and fiction. *Therapeutic Advances in Respiratory Disease, 3*(3), 131-141. https://doi.org/10.1177/1753465809340571

Stone, J., Carson, A., & Sharpe, M. (2005). Functional symptoms in neurology: Management. *BMJ Journals, 76*(suppl_1), i13-i21. https://doi.org/10.1136/jnnp.2004.061663

Suni, E., & Dimitriu, A. (2020, October 30). *Dreams: Why we dream & how they affect sleep.* Sleep Foundation. https://www.sleepfoundation.org/dreams

This is how much sweat you lose each hour in extreme heat. (2017, July 5). KHQ Right Now. https://www.khq.com/news/this-is-how-much-sweat-you-lose-each-hour-in-extreme-heat/article_15717480-f697-58f7-b9bf-c0feb5964b85.html

Trudeau, M., & Greenhalgh, J. (2017, May 15). *Yawning may promote social bonding even between dogs and humans.* NPR. https://www.npr.org/sections/health-shots/2017/05/15/527106576/yawning-may-promote-social-bonding-even-between-dogs-and-humans

Understanding microphones. (2012, June 27). Institute of Museum and Library. https://ohda.matrix.msu.edu/2012/06/understanding-microphones/

Uttekar, P. S. (n.d.). *How much does an average person sweat in a day?* Medicine-Net. https://www.medicinenet.com/how_much_does_an_average_person_sweat_in_a_day/article.htm

Uvula: Anatomy, function & definition. (2022, April 6). Cleveland Clinic. https://my.clevelandclinic.org/health/body/22674-uvula

Van, G. (2018, May 31). *Does coffee really stunt your growth?* Healthline. https://www.healthline.com/nutrition/does-coffee-stunt-growth

van de Laar, L. (2022, May 17). Sneezing: 10 reasons, causes, and triggers. *Houston ENT.* https://www.houstonent.com/blog/sneezing-10-reasons-causes-and-triggers

Vandergriendt, C. (2023, March 20). *How long can you go without sleep? Function, hallucination, more.* Healthline. https://www.healthline.com/health/healthy-sleep/how-long-can-you-go-without-sleep

Villazon, L. (n.d.). *Why does sneezing feel so good?* Science Focus. https://www.sciencefocus.com/the-human-body/why-does-sneezing-feel-so-good

Wells, D. (2017, November 20). *Phantosmia: Smoke, other common smells, causes, treatment.* Healthline. https://www.healthline.com/health/phantosmia

What attracts mosquitoes? Understanding the factors that draw them in. (2024, September 23). Aptive Environmental. https://aptivepestcontrol.com/pests/mosquitoes/what-attracts-mosquitoes-understanding-the-factors-that-draw-them-in/

What happens if you hold in farts? (n.d.). Hackensack Meridian Health. https://www.hackensackmeridianhealth.org/en/healthu/2023/11/15/what-happens-if-you-hold-in-farts

Whelan, C. (2020, September 22). *Why do onions make you cry? Enzymes, treatments & more.* Healthline. https://www.healthline.com/health/why-do-onions-make-you-cry

Whitcomb, I. (2022, July 18). *Why do we get goosebumps?* Live Science. https://www.livescience.com/32349-what-causes-goose-bumps.html

Why are people ticklish? (2024, May 30). Cleveland Clinic. https://health.clevelandclinic.org/why-are-people-ticklish

Why do I remember useless information over useful information? (2018). The Naked Scientists. https://www.thenakedscientists.com/articles/questions/why-do-i-remember-useless-information-over-useful-information

Why do we laugh when someone falls over? (2011, February 14). University of Cambridge. https://www.cam.ac.uk/news/why-do-we-laugh-when-someone-falls-over

Why do we like our own farts? (2014, November 9). ScienceAlert. https://www.sciencealert.com/watch-why-do-we-like-our-own-farts

Why do we sneeze? (2021, June 16). Williams Integracare Clinic. https://integracareclinics.com/why-do-we-sneeze/

Why do your ears pop in planes? (2025). Royal Society Te Apārangi. https://www.royalsociety.org.nz/150th-anniversary/ask-me-questions/why-do-your-ears-pop-in-planes/

Why do your ears pop on an airplane? And other flying questions answered. (2022, August 5). BBC Bitesize. https://www.bbc.co.uk/bitesize/articles/zvcd7v4

Why does my body jerk before I fall asleep? (for teens). (n.d.). Nemours Teens Health. https://kidshealth.org/en/teens/sleep-start.html

Why does my foot fall asleep? (for kids). (2025). Kids Health. https://kidshealth.org/en/kids/foot-asleep.html

Why does your voice sound different on a recording? (2013, September 14). *BBC*. https://www.bbc.com/future/article/20130913-why-we-hate-hearing-our-own-voice

Why we remember trivia: The science of memory. (2024, October 21). *The Sporcle Blog*. https://www.sporcle.com/blog/2024/10/why-we-remember-trivia/

Winchester, S. (2003). *Krakatoa: The day the world exploded.* Harper Collins.

Zoppi, L. (2020, July 17). *What to know about morning breath.* Medical News Today. https://www.medicalnewstoday.com/articles/morning-breath

www.ingramcontent.com/pod-product-compliance
Lightning Source LLC
Chambersburg PA
CBHW060240030426
42335CB00014B/1550